THIS IS YOUR TIME

THIS
IS
YOUR
TIME

RUBY BRIDGES

AN IMPRINT OF PUSHKIN PRESS

Pushkin Press
71–75 Shelton Street
London WC2H 9JQ

Text © 2020 Ruby Bridges

Published by arrangement with Random House Children's Books,
a division of Penguin Random House LLC

Some photographs are from the author's collection.
Remaining image credits are located on pages 56 and 57.

This is Your Time was first published by Delacorte Press in New York, 2020

First published by Pushkin Press in 2021

1 3 5 7 9 8 6 4 2

ISBN 13: 978-1-91159-059-0

Jacket art: Original art from *The Problem We All Live With*
is in the collection of the Norman Rockwell Museum, Stockbridge, MA.

Image courtesy of the Norman Rockwell Museum.

Interior design by Stephanie Moss

Offset by Tetragon, London
Printed and bound in Great Britain by TJ Books, Padstow, Cornwall

www.pushkinpress.com

I dedicate this "letter of peace" to Congressman John Lewis,
icon of the civil rights movement, with admiration.
He was known as the conscience of Congress,
truly an example of
"a soul generated by love."

Job well done, our good and faithful servant!
The torch is passed!

We have much work to do,
Young Peacemakers of the World. . . .

To the young peacemakers of the world,

Sixty years ago, in 1960, my life changed forever. Although I was not aware of it, my country was changing too. What I remember about that time, through my six-year-old eyes, is that there was extreme unrest, much like we see today. I was chosen to be the first black child to go to an all-white school, William Frantz Elementary, in my hometown, New Orleans.

I did not yet know that I had stepped into the history books.

The 1954 U.S. Supreme Court decision in Brown v. Board of Education *deemed racial segregation in schools unconstitutional.*

For my whole first-grade year I had to be escorted to and from school by four federal marshals, under the order of the president of the United States, because people were afraid for my safety.

U.S. marshals escort Ruby Bridges from William Frantz Elementary School in New Orleans in November 1960.

Going into and coming out of school every day, I walked through crowds of people yelling, screaming threats, throwing things at six-year-old me. They were against the integration of black and white children in the same school. I had been so excited to meet and make new friends at school, and was met with something utterly different and terrifying.

Angry segregationist protesters gathered daily outside Ruby's school (1960).

It was a difficult decision for both of my parents to agree to let me go to school along with the marshals, especially for my dad, but they knew it was necessary. My father, like most dads, wanted nothing more than to protect his little girl. But as a young black man, it was not safe for him to walk me to school.

Police officers flank the entrance for Ruby's arrival on her first day (1960).

My father loved me more than I would ever know, and I felt that he was my very own hero.

Ruby and her father, Abon Bridges (1960).

He was also a real hero, having received a Purple Heart for bravery while serving overseas in the Korean War. But he did not return to a hero's welcome. There was little work given to young black men back then.

Ruby's father, a Korean War veteran, in uniform.

When I arrived at this all-white school that first day, all the white parents rushed in and pulled out their kids. They didn't want their children going to school with me. But why? I didn't understand. They had never met or even seen me before now, so how could they know what kind of person I was? But none of that mattered. I don't think they even saw a child. All they saw was the color of my skin. I was black, and that meant I didn't matter.

Some teachers even quit their jobs because they didn't want to teach black children.

Parents outside William Frantz Elementary School carry a coffin holding a black doll as they protest integration (1960).

14

My teacher, Barbara Henry, came all the way from Boston to teach me. For the entire year she sat alone with me in that classroom and taught me everything I needed to know. She really made school fun. We never missed a day that whole year. We knew we had to be at school for each other.

Ruby and her teacher, Barbara Henry. Though the school was desegregated, white parents refused to let their children share a classroom with Ruby (1960).

I felt safe and loved, and that was because of Mrs. Henry, who, by the way, looked exactly like the women in that screaming mob outside. But she wasn't like them. She showed me her heart, and even at six years old I knew she was different. Barbara Henry was white and I was black, and we mattered to each other. She became my best friend. I knew that if I got safely past the angry crowd outside and into my classroom, I was going to have a good day.

Ruby reunites with Barbara Henry at the unveiling of a statue in Ruby's honor at William Frantz Elementary School (2014).

Outside of that classroom, the world seemed a very violent place. I later learned that those people in the mob had hatred toward me solely because of the color of my skin.

Top: Protesters gather at William Frantz Elementary School (1960); bottom: A crowd of teenagers is dispersed by police outside integrated William Frantz Elementary School (1960).

I thought often of the lessons of Dr. Martin Luther King, Jr., who gave his life trying to teach us to judge people "not by the color of their skin but by the content of their character." Truly these people did not agree with him.

Dr. Martin Luther King, Jr. (first row, third from right), with other civil rights leaders and supporters at the March on Washington on August 28, 1963.

Our elders said back then that if black folks really wanted to see change, they had to step up to the plate and do it themselves. Somebody had to be first—but because I was first, my father was fired from his job.

Clockwise from upper left: Signs indicate enforcement of segregation laws, also known as Jim Crow laws; picketers march against discriminatory business practices; more than 250,000 people attend the March on Washington to demand racial equality; Bayard Rustin (left) and Cleveland Robinson (right), two of the organizers of the march.

NO DOGS NEGROES MEXICANS

LONESTAR RESTAURANT ASSN. Dallas, Texas

REST ROOMS
ITE COLORED →

L&N

COLORED
EATED IN REAR

The PRESENCE OF SEGREGATION IS THE ABSENCE OF DEMOCRACY
JIM CROW MUST GO!

NATIONAL HEADQUARTERS
MARCH ON **WASHINGTON** FOR **JOBS** & **FREEDOM**
WED. AUG. 28

Over the last twenty-five years I've had the honor of meeting so many of you in person in your schools as I've traveled across the country and around the world. In your faces and through our interactions I have seen innocence, love, respect, kindness, and sometimes even sadness.

Ruby Bridges speaks to schoolchildren around the world.

I recall once meeting little Megan, who said that I was truly her hero and that because I'm so brave, she had to be brave like me; she had to seek help because her father was abusing her mom. Megan is truly a testament to bravery in the midst of sadness.

Children have long played an important role in the movement for social justice, as shown by these young activists in the late 1950s.

And young Ryan, who explained how we're all the same, just like his puppy, Rex. His golden retriever is strong and fast and does awesome tricks, and he loves it more than anything. Jimmy, Ryan's best friend, has a collie that is black with white spots. It is not quite as fast as Ryan's dog, but it is smarter. Jimmy loves his dog too. Yes, the dogs are different, but they are both loved. Both are just dogs— the same.

I see that as a true expression of love and respect.

Young people all over the world are raising their voices to demand change.

Another time, I met Vae, who said we are all like a bag of M&M's—different on the outside, but the same inside. Gotta love those M&M's.

Ruby Bridges with new friends a few months into her attendance at William Frantz Elementary School in New Orleans (1961).

I have not witnessed hatred or bigotry when I've looked into your young eyes. Regardless of what you looked like or where you came from, I saw some of my six-year-old self in you. You did not care about the color of each other's skin, and I have loved seeing that because I saw hope. Hope that most people don't get a chance to see, and I thank you for sharing that.

With the growth of the Black Lives Matter movement, more and more children are participating in public demonstrations, like this one in the Netherlands in June 2020.

I have been saying for many years how I believe racism is a grown-up disease, and we "adults" must stop using you, our kids, to spread it. None of you is born into the world racist. It is we adults who pass racism on. In so many ways, we have failed you by not setting the example you deserve. I have always believed it is our role as grown-ups to guide, lead, and teach our children . . . to set the best example . . . just as you must do as you grow up.

Young peacemakers of America hope for a bright future.

As I've watched events unfold over these many years, and especially since May 2020, I am reminded of the strength and resilience of young people. I agonize over the horrific violence we see over and over against black people.

Top: A water cannon is aimed at young African Americans during a protest in Birmingham, Alabama (1963).
Bottom: Officers shoot pepper spray during a demonstration after the death of George Floyd, whose murder at the hands of police sparked outrage around the world (2020).

My heart aches because I know the reality of the world we are living in today. I am a black mother of four black sons. My eldest son, Craig, was murdered.

Family members grieve at the funeral of Freddie Gray, who died in police custody in 2015.

The loss of any child, no matter their age, is a parent's worst nightmare. Such a loss does destroy families. I feel your pain. My heart goes out to all those who have experienced black lives lost. Those lives had meaning and purpose to their families, so indeed, they mattered.

Ruby's son Craig Hall and his family in 1996. Craig lost his life in a random shooting in New Orleans in 2005.

When I think about how great my country could be—America, land of the free, home of the brave—I think about what Dr. Martin Luther King, Jr., said about being great: "Everybody can be great, because everybody can serve. . . .

The spirit of Reverend Dr. Martin Luther King, Jr., continues to inspire all those who work for peace and justice.

"You only need a heart full of grace."

Really, it is that love and grace for one another that will heal this world.

It is that love and grace that will allow us to see one another as brothers and sisters.

It is that love and grace that will allow us to respect the many ways God has made all of us unique and will allow us to turn our stumbling blocks into stepping-stones.

A show of solidarity at a rally in front of city hall in Baltimore, Maryland, following widespread riots (2015).

Stepping-stones toward the America we know we can be. United, one nation under God, indivisible, with liberty and justice for all.

Demonstrators hug during a march in Los Angeles in response to George Floyd's death (2020).

Protests continue in streets across America and far beyond. I am so inspired by you and by everyone out there making change happen. I know, and you must remember . . . what can inspire tomorrow often lies in our past.

Top: Civil rights leader John Lewis (foreground) is beaten by an Alabama state trooper during the first Selma-to-Montgomery march (1965). Bottom: A demonstrator kneels and raises her hands facing a police line in front of the White House while participating in a Black Lives Matter rally (2020).

May my past, my story, inspire you. The first steps toward change are never easy, but six-year-old Ruby Bridges taught us that it is necessary to take those steps.

Ruby Bridges (1960).

Don't be afraid. This is your time in history. Keep your eyes on the prize. And at all costs, stay united.

Ruby B

Ruby Bridges delivers the commencement address at Rhode Island College (2019).

IMAGE CREDITS

Page 43: From the author's collection

Page 45: AP Images

Page 47: Nicholas Kamm/Getty Images

Page 49: Brent Stirton/Getty Images

Page 51: (top) AP Images; (bottom) Samuel Corum/Getty Images

Page 53: Paul Slade/Getty Images

Page 55: *The Providence Journal*/Kris Craig

Pages 56-57: WE AS ONE copyright © 1981 by Gilbert Young

Page 58: From the author's collection

The jacket of *This Is Your Time* features a portion of *The Problem We All Live With,* Norman Rockwell's 1964 painting of Ruby's historic walk to school. The painting is considered an iconic image of the civil rights movement in the United States.

The Problem We All Live With was originally published as a centerfold in the January 14, 1964, issue of *Look* magazine. Rockwell had ended his contract with the *Saturday Evening Post* the previous year due to frustration with the limits the magazine placed on his expression of political themes, and *Look* offered him a forum for his social interests, including civil rights and racial integration.

ACKNOWLEDGMENTS

I'd like to acknowledge and thank all my babies, the schoolkids I've spoken to over these past twenty-five years. You've shown me your heart.